Changing the Game: What You are Doing Doesn't Work Anymore

Rhondra O. Willis, Ph.D.

Copyright © 2012 Nicole Group, Inc.
All rights reserved.
ISBN -10: 0615653839
ISBN-13: 978-0615653839

DEDICATION

This book is dedicated to my wonderful parents, James M. Willis (SMSGT, RET) and Mrs. Sherrill Willis. God didn't have to but He gave me His very best when He gave me the two of you. Dad: Our daily talks during my time at the Academy and while you were fighting for your life strengthened ME. You always told me to "push myself" and you led by example. Mom: Your perfect and unfailing love through God kept me sane and kept me on track. Our long talks stabilized me and provided a much-needed anchor in a terrible storm. You are truly a Proverbs 31 Woman.

Marvin, I love your quiet strength and calm reserve, for it propels you past where many people would stop short and give up.

Debra, I love your creative spirit; feed it and it will grow and take you to places you never imagined or dared dream.

Nicole, you were not with us for long but God blessed us with you. You may not physically be here, but your spirit and legacy lives on through us. You live forever in our hearts.

Dianett and Sandra, I will simply say thank you for blazing the trail for my independence and stepping in when Nicole had to step out.

CONTENTS

ACKNOWLEDGMENTS..5

CREATING YOUR OWN URGENCY SHARPENS YOUR FOCUS...7

BE A FINISHER..8

CREATE SPACE..9

FOR SUCH A TIME AS THIS.......................................10

GET IN WHERE YOU FIT IN..11

THRIVE WHERE YOU ARRIVE 13

WOMAN INTERRUPTED..14

SECRET WEAPONS.. 15

CONDITIONING 16

DEVELOP TENACIOUS-ABILITY................................18

THERE IS SAFETY IN NUMBERS 20

ABC - ACCURACY BUILDS CREDIBILITY ©..............22

STAY FOCUSED - IT'S PERSONAL 24

ACKNOWLEDGMENTS

Aunt Blanche, Uncle Grady, Aunt Jackie, and Unkie (Dr. Hill): I love you and thank you for all that you did for me throughout my journey. You are so special to me. God truly dealt me a winning hand.

To my sister-in-law, Canada, to my nieces and nephews: Kyla, Brianna, Kameron, Kris, Kien, Ryan, and Jaquin - Dream BIG. It's all possible.

Nicole Wilder: My best friend since sixth grade. You taught me not to fear my dreams but to live them!

Mama Walker: You will always hold a very special place in place in my heart. I love you.

Mama (Reverend) Champaign: You are another amazing woman in my life. Keep on keeping on!

Bishop Lyle and Pastor Debra Dukes: Thank you for being my Shepherds while I am far away from home. May God continue to bless you and the Household of Faith – Harvest Life Changers Church.

Demar Roberts: I love you and thank you. You inspire me and I am in awe watching how God works in your life.

JS: You held my hand throughout this story.

MA: Thank you for your kindness. You do not know the depth of my gratitude.

(Dr.) Wanda Corner: All I can say is "How Great is our God!" We met by chance, no by divine design, and the rest is HERstory.

CG and TD: You are my mentors by divine design. I thank God for your willingness to give much needed guidance and support during a critical point in my life. Your strength is amazing!

DE: You taught me more than you will ever know.

MR: You arrived in the midst of the storm and showed me my value when I needed it most. Thank you.

FOREWORD

Dr. Willis, a one-time federal agent trainee, reassigned to Headquarters after failing firearms qualifications, chronicled her experiences over the last three years in *Changing the Game*. In biblical terms and significance, the number three is a number of completion. Dr. Willis believes she came full circle by God's grace and mercy.

The intent of this book is to share hope and love with others who find themselves in a similar situation. This book is her testimony that God is able AND willing to deliver His people from the hands of the enemy. We experience adversity to help us grow and mature – people who we believe are most challenging in our lives are our greaTEST gifts. They are divinely assigned to usher us to the next level. Your circumstances may not change but YOU will change! His grace IS sufficient. Embrace it!

----

0 4 ∞ 2 7 ∞ 0 9

Results of God's Creation
Sovereignty and Divine Completion
God's Judgment
God's Perfect Plan

0 4 ∞ 2 7 ∞ 1 2

CREATING YOUR OWN URGENCY SHARPENS YOUR FOCUS

While I floundered and almost stalled during a crucial point of my quantitative analysis while completing my dissertation, I realized that by creating URGENCY with those who were part of the process, my seeming inability to move was suddenly lurching forward and launching me into where I wanted and needed to be…

∞ **REFLECTIONS** ∞

_____

_____

_____

_____

BE A FINISHER

As we strive to become more Christ-like, we need to remember that He who started a good work in us is able to accomplish it… (Philippians 1:6). Life happens and you often start projects that fall by the wayside, but as you begin to Change the Game, leverage your unFINISHed business into making it your business. Those articles that you started to write, revive them and find a venue to share your message. The website that you started to build, revamp it and get started! Breathe new life into stale projects! Remember the race is not given to those who are swift and FINISH first, but to those who stay in the race and fight the good fight of faith (Ecclesiastes 9:11)!

CREATE SPACE

Has the Lord ever woken you up in the middle of the night and shared His heart with you through ideas and insights? Why does He wake us up at night? Many times, it is because that is the only time that we are still and can hear Him speak.

I am striving to CREATE SPACE through prayer, quiet time, meditation, and reflection – you will find when you clear the clutter – the critical masses will push to the front of the line. Commit to living a clutter-free life in the physical and the spiritual.

∞ **REFLECTIONS** ∞

_____

_____

_____

FOR SUCH A TIME AS THIS...

Esther was forever etched into history as she prepared to meet her destiny and her calling by declaring, "…. If I perish, then I perish" (Esther 4:16). She realized her time was NOW and that she was in the moment.

This was a difficult concept for me, always striving for "when" – when is NOW. I often missed great opportunities because I was looking beyond (not a negative attitude), but I still needed to see the trees and not just the forest. Please do not misunderstand; the big picture IS important, but let us live in the NOW. Being present in the immediate moment is key to reaching our goals and dreams.

GET IN WHERE YOU FIT IN

Not so long ago, I was thrown, no pushed, into a situation where I was moved out of the mainstream of activity into a seemingly obscure one. I was confused, hurt, and I couldn't understand why I felt like I was being pushed out of my position. I refused to participate in the "game" by stepping on other people and forgetting the basic tenants of human dignity and respect. Employing the "golden rule" had always worked for me before – why not now?

When you live in a place like this one – remember – man's rejection is God's protection. He never makes mistakes and will keep you if you do not forsake His ways or commandments. "Your gift will make room for you" (Proverbs 18:16). By honoring God, you are sowing a seed (remember the spiritual and natural laws of sowing and reaping). God will honor you, and He will exalt you in due time (1 Peter 5:6). The key here is to rejoice in your "suffering" – count it all joy (James 1:2) – and REST assured that God is working it out for your good (Romans 8:28).

"Do not allow the enemy to grieve you about issues that are not about you or tied to your destiny"

∞ REFLECTIONS ∞

_____

_____

_____

_____

_____

_____

THRIVE WHERE YOU ARRIVE

Sometimes we end up in places that we never wanted to live or even visit, but when God has a lesson for you to master – you will be there until you learn the lesson and He releases you.

Lessons come to purify us and prepare us for the next level. Purification can be painful and the fire intense. When you come through the fire, you will be refined, purified, and prepared to move forward, but not UNTIL you master the lesson.

∞ **REFLECTIONS** ∞

_____

_____

_____

_____

WOMAN INTERRUPTED

When you feel stagnant, you may be tempted to accept distractions of places, things, or people that are contrary to your destination. Distractions remain just that – DIS tractions; they make you lose traction in your journey. This is why it is important to CREATE SPACE and stay focused. Losing your FOCUS is detrimental to your journey and will cause you to stay in the valley longer than you wish to endure.

When facing something or someone new, do not just accept what or who is presented but try the Spirit by the Spirit (1 John 2:4), and you will truly see the hand of God. If you are INTERRUPTED or distracted, do not despair, just immerse yourself in CREATING SPACE and you will see the clearing again in due time.

SECRET WEAPONS

The government classifies information into different categories including SECRET, which generally means that you cannot share this information with everyone because revealing too much information to the general public or mortal enemies is detrimental to national security.

God will draw you into SECRET places (Isaiah 45:3) – You have been cleared (proven and tried) and "read in" by virtue of the blood-bought right of Jesus Christ. By CREATING SPACE and drawing nigh to God (James 4:8), you will live in the NOW, and He will develop SECRET WEAPONS in and for you that will give you the advantage and (a supernatural) edge.

CONDITIONING

When I started running again after taking a very long hiatus after college, I struggled to run just a few minutes without gasping for air, and my legs were screaming in pain. Now I run several miles with no problems. I used to wonder how people just ran without gasping for air or having to stop because of pain. The answer is CONDITIONING.

We CONDITION many things: our hair, our bodies, our cars, and on and on. CONDITIONING is important because it prepares us for the journey that lies ahead. CONDITIONING allows us to push beyond the break. My dad always likes to say that you have to push yourself. Pushing requires an opposite and forceful action against pressure. This is how he mentally CONDITIONS himself to push forward when it seems mentally or physically challenging or impossible. CONDITIONING is what happens before the real work or journey ever occurs.

"When it seems you are drowning, it may be that the waters have risen to cleanse you not consume you. The storm will pass"

∞ REFLECTIONS ∞

_____

_____

_____

_____

_____

_____

_____

DEVELOP TENACIOUS-ABILITY

My supervisor was always telling me that I was TENACIOUS. I knew what that meant on the surface, but I like to look up words to understand the full definition and meaning. I wanted to go beyond my surface understanding.

When I looked up TENACIOUS, I learned that it meant not easily separated… That meant something to me – I latched on to it. We are not easily, in fact, NOTHING can separate us from the love of Christ (Romans 8:38-39). His love will protect us in all situations and environments. We are to be confident in all situations, even if it does not look promising – fear not, God is TENACIOUS concerning His children and His promises.

Our mission in trying situations is to hold fast to His promises and activate our faith. We can always rest in the fact that He is working it all out for our good and benefit (Romans 8:28).

∞ REFLECTIONS ∞

_____

_____

_____

_____

_____

_____

_____

_____

_____

_____

_____

THERE IS SAFETY IN NUMBERS

CREATE allies, genuine allies – allies that will support you and ones you can support. Understand that people will come and go in your life. That is part of life, and God speaks of this in the scriptures: "They went out from us, but they were not really of us; for if they had been of us, they would have remained with us; but they went out, so that it would be shown that they all are not of us" (1 John 2:19); and "No doubt there have to be differences among you to show which of you have God's approval" (1 Corinthians 11:19).

When "friends" leave, it is by divine appointment and design. We may not ever understand it but trust me, we can trust God. He knows what is best and has already ordered your steps (Proverbs 4:12).

∞ **REFLECTIONS** ∞

_____

_____

_____

_____

_____

_____

_____

_____

_____

"Your success can't be measured by anyone else. You have to set your own goals and do what gives you a sense of fulfillment"

ABC
ACCURACY BUILDS CREDIBILITY©

Accuracy Builds Credibility. This is a fundamental lesson, and I learned it the hard way. In my previous environment, I never questioned the information that I received from a third party, but in my new environment, I learned this lesson through my dismay and to my detriment.

As I regained holy boldness and confidence, I began a renewed pursuit of ACCURACY. This involved seeking knowledge and investing in a hunger for growth where I once was stagnant. Today this process continues as a daily pursuit of mind renewal of not just spiritual, but natural knowledge. "Do not conform to the pattern of this world, but be transformed by the renewing of your mind. Then you will be able to test and approve what God's will is —His good, pleasing and perfect will" (Romans 12:2). Further, "You will seek me and find me when you seek me with all your heart" (Jeremiah 29:13).

Continue to run the race and allow God to prune you through His grace and correction made evident through the knowledge of His Word.

∞ REFLECTIONS ∞

_____

_____

_____

_____

_____

Quote from Jim Rohn, America's Foremost Business Philosopher, reprinted with permission from Jim Rohn International ©2011.

STAY FOCUSED - IT'S PERSONAL

One negative habit (habits are routine thoughts/behaviors that we compulsively carry out in response to events in our lives) that plagued me over the last three years was to lose sight of God and His plan for my life. I often wanted to look at what was happening in lives of others and, in comparing my life with theirs, it is easy to forget that the events in my life are PERSONAL. This is between me and God - He KNEW me before the very foundation of the earth. Therefore, when you find yourself off course because you are not minding your own business and staying YOUR course, remember this tip that my trainer gave me - I often struggle with balance (physical and work), but when we are doing balancing exercises my trainer tells me to find a focal point (God) and keep my eyes on it. She is right for, when I focus; I can balance and achieve my goals. When I look around, and I am not minding my own business - I lose my focus, my edge.

When this challenge raises its ugly head, I engage (commit to it, no matter the circumstances) in self-talk. I recently bought a new car, and every time I drift over the line without using my signal, the car beeps and tells me to get back in line. Likewise, when I begin to look at other people and what is going on in their lives versus what is going in my life, I begin to talk to myself, remind myself to FOCUS, and mind my own business.

Seasons are natural and are part of God's plans in the natural and in the supernatural world. Winter comes to give bears an opportunity to hibernate while other creatures are active, but the bears anticipate, expect, and accept the impending season, whether it is summer or winter, and they prepare themselves. This is part of their natural activities and their life cycle. As children of God, we should begin to embrace changing seasons as part of our life cycle, but we should never lose hope in God's Divine and Sovereign Plan for our lives. "We are His workmanship . . . which God prepared beforehand. . ."(Eph. 2:10).

"Sometimes we hold onto something so long that it becomes a matter of principle not purpose. Let it go"

∞ REFLECTIONS ∞

_____

_____

_____

_____

ABOUT THE AUTHOR

DR. RHONDRA O. WILLIS is the newest **EAR: E**ducator, **A**uthor, and **R**esearcher in the inspirational arena. She is the emergent author of *Changing the Game: What You are Doing Doesn't Work Anymore,* a pocketbook to equip, to empower, to encourage, and to inspire her readers. Changing the Game offers strategies to survive and thrive in the midst of challenging environments.

As an innovator in nonprofit development, resource building, business and strategic management, she is President and CEO of Nicole Group, Inc., – a full-service business management consulting and publishing company. Nicole Group, Inc. also houses the Center for Social Entrepreneurship designed to facilitate social enterprise in a capitalist-driven society.

In 2000, she founded Vision Leadership Institute, a non-profit organization that provides health education services, leadership development, and academic enrichment for at-risk youth and women. The Institute has partnered with the United States Department of Health and Human Services (Office of Woman's Health), to provide HIV/AIDS prevention services.

Dr. Willis has been involved in numerous projects and committees for various organizations to include: DIVA International, United States Department of Health and Services, South Carolina Department of Health and Environmental Control (DHEC), American Association of University Women, the Medical University of South Carolina, University of South Carolina's Business Division Research Division, National Institutes of Health (New Investigator Program), Richland County Business Service Center Appeals Board, Allen University, and University of South Carolina's Women's Studies Initiative.

Dr. Willis firmly believes: *"To whom much is given – much is required."*

For more information visit rhondrawillis.com

www.ingramcontent.com/pod-product-compliance
Lightning Source LLC
Chambersburg PA
CBHW060623070426
42449CB00042B/2485